Published by Pastoral Educational Services
Special Projects Division of
Paulist Press
400 Sette Drive, Paramus, New Jersey 07652

President: Rev. Kevin A. Lynch, C.S.P.
Vice President and Project Director:
Rev. Thomas E. Comber, C.S.P.

Editor and Photographic Selection: Joseph W. Nash
Production Assistant: Miss Rae Fronzaglia

Design: Ron Cutro Associates, Tenafly, N. J.

Picture Credits:
Lou Niznik—Cover, End Sheets and Pages: 9, 13, 14, 23, 24,
26-27, 31, 37, 38-39, 42, 44-45, 68, 81, 84
Tony Roberts—Pages: 3, 58-59
Peter Lange—Pages: 74-75, 76-77, 90-91
Donald Abrams—Pages: 40-41, 88-89
Sister Diane Smith—Pages: 73, 92-93
Ray Gora—Pages: 20-21, 50-51
George Hoffmann—Page: 49
George and Richard Egley: Pages 4-5
Joseph A. Nash—Pages: 66-67
A. B. Arluke—Pages: 82-83
Ted Hoffmann—Pages: 46-47
Michael Kloczkowicz—Pages: 16-17, 62
Audrey Merchant—Pages: 70-71
(Black Star)
    Doug Wilson—Pages: 18, 78-79
    John Launois—Pages: 64-65
    Dan McCoy—Pages: 6, 10-11
    Mike Mauney—Page: 28
    Don Rutledge—Page 54
    C. Vanderberg—Pages: 32-33
    A. Gruen—Page: 57
    Ernest Baxter—Pages: 52-53

Library of Congress
Catalog Card Number: 72-75632

Color Separations by:
Color Control Corp., Little Ferry, N. J.

Printed and bound in the
United States of America by:
R. R. Donnelly & Sons Co., Chicago, Ill.
G.T.O. Lithographers, Inc., Little Ferry, N. J.

Copyright © 1972 by
The Missionary Society
of St. Paul the Apostle
in the State of New York

The Scriptural selections have been taken from two
sources. Identification of sources is indicated
below by page numbers. Where two meditations are
on one page the *left* references will be the page
numbers, the *right* references will have an A after
the page numbers.

Excerpts from *The Jerusalem Bible,* copyright © 1966
by Darton, Longman & Todd, Ltd. and Doubleday and
Company, Inc. Used by permission of the publisher.
Jerusalem Bible references: Pages: 11, 15, 16, 19,
19A, 22A, 25A, 27, 29A, 30A, 33, 41, 48, 51, 56A,
59, 61A, 66, 77, 79, 87, 87A, 88, 89, 90

Excerpts from *The Complete Bible: An American
Translation* edited and translated by John Merlin
Powis Smith and Edgar J. Goodspeed, copyright
© 1923, 1927, 1948 by The University of Chicago.
Used by permission of the publisher.
The Complete Bible: An American Translation
references: Pages: 7, 7A, 8, 8A, 12, 12A, 15A, 20,
21, 22, 25, 29, 30, 32, 34, 34A, 35, 35A, 36, 36A, 38,
43, 43A, 44, 45, 47, 48A, 52, 53, 55, 55A, 56, 60,
60A, 61, 63, 63A, 65, 69, 69A, 70, 72, 75, 76, 80,
80A, 82, 82A, 85, 85A, 86, 86A, 91, 92

Note: where Scripture is used within a reflection
the location in the Bible is shown immediately below.

Excerpts used in meditations on pages 43 (left),
72, and 75 are from *Report To Greco* by Nikos
Kazantazakis © 1965 by Simon and Schuster.
Used by permission of the publisher.

Reflections
...path to prayer

by JAMES TURRO

Foreword

Faith is a way of seeing,
an eye
for looking out on life
and the universe.
To look upon the world
in faith
is to discover there,
new and unsuspected dimensions
that link the world
with God.
Such discoveries
can open
a path to prayer.

I earnestly hope
that it may be so
in the experience
of all
who take up this book.
I should like to think
that the reflections
contained herein
may create for the reader
a moment of pure,
if fragile
and fleeting,
insight
that will take him
where he otherwise
might not go:
to God
—along a path of prayer.

4

"O God
who made the beautiful earth
when will it be ready to
receive thy Saints?"
Words from
Shaw's 'St. Joan' that
decry the unseeing coldness
of the world.
Words of subtle comfort
for those who try to walk
in Christ's way today.
For there should be
no cause for surprise
that good men are ignored,
or worse yet, persecuted
—for this is
the *way* of the world.
No cause for surprise
that your good intentions
are too often misread;
that you yourself
are unappreciated
in the good works you try to do—
for *this*
is the way of the world.

The world crucified Christ,
mocked His good works
and tried to stifle
His truth and mission;
but Christ is *fully* alive
and the Christian message
is more powerful than ever before.

You may be persecuted or
misunderstood, ridiculed,
ignored or assaulted
but, remember, your efforts,
your work, will live on long after
those who mocked are gone.

You will be hated by everybody on my account, but
the man who holds out to the very end will be saved.
(Matthew 10:22)

So often
the persons called by God
to his special work
have had to leave home.
This was certainly true of
Abraham, Joseph, Moses and Ruth.

To be sure
leaving home for these four
implied more than a physical transfer
from one place to another.
It meant
leaving a familiar context of life
with its own pattern of thinking,
with its
traditional values and viewpoints.
It meant
going over to
a new mode of life and thought.

No less a break
with one's environment
is expected today of the person
called to God's work.

Have you left home?

If anyone comes to me without hating his own father
and mother and wife and children and brothers
and sisters, and his very life too,
he cannot be a disciple of mine.
(Luke 14:26)

"The very hairs
on your heads
are all counted!"†
—an unusual way of saying
a most soothing truth.

By these words
Christ has wanted
to say:
God cares
for you
with a deep-down
care;
one
that exceeds
your own concern
for yourself.
God
has a more detailed
and intimate knowledge
of you
than you yourself possess.
For even you
do not have
so passionate an interest
in yourself
as to
have taken a count
of the hairs
on your head.

†Luke 12:7

Then will not God provide protection for his
chosen people, who cry out to him day and night?
Is he slow to help them? I tell you,
he will make haste to provide it!
(Luke 18:7-8)

There is
a vehement passion in man
that propels him
unremittingly
toward God.
In these days,
this drive, as it appears,
is inarticulate
and, at best, is
only dimly realized.
No one goes about professing
an urge toward God.

Yet this aspiration
for all its
wordlessness and for all
its being staunchly disavowed
is strong and real.

The disquiet
and general want
of social ease
that one senses widely in the world
may be read
as a symptom
of man's breathless,
groping struggle
toward God.

"You have made our hearts
for Thee
and they will not rest
until they rest
in Thee."†

†St. Augustine

As a deer longs for the water-courses,
so my whole being longs for thee, O God.
(Psalm 42:1)

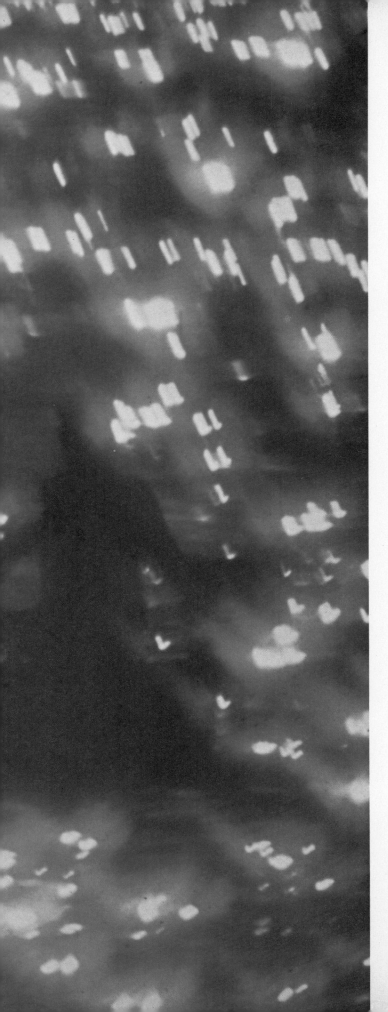

The same word
    that Christ spoke to Peter
He has spoken to you:
"Come."
Come out onto the sea
of religious life
with all its risks
and uncertainties.

Take special note
of the word "Come."
Christ did not say "go."
Thus when we
embark on our religious adventure
we do not move *away*
("go.")
but *toward* him all the while.
("Come.")
So whatever anguish,
whatever pain
lurks out there
in the deep,
this much at least is true:
Christ is there
to support you.

That is why I am telling you not to worry about
your life and what you are to eat, nor about
your body and how you are to clothe it. . . .
Your Father well knows you need them.
No; set your hearts on his kingdom, and
these other things will be given you as well.
(Luke 12:22-31)

C hrist has been defined as
GOD'S AMEN.
A curious phrase.
"Amen" means "yes".

To what
has God said "yes"
in sending us Christ?
"Yes" to our best hopes.
"Yes" to our struggle
for peace.
"Yes" to our soaring desire
to grow.

How just it is
to say and sing
of Bethlehem
as we do each year at Christmas:
"the joys and fears
of all the years are
met in thee tonight."
For in Bethlehem
on the first Christmas,
God uttered a beautiful Word.
That Word was
his Son.
That Word was
"no" to our fears,
"yes" to our joys.

See! God's dwelling is with men, and he will live with
them. They will be his people and God himself will
be with them, and he will wipe every tear from
their eyes. There will be no death any longer,
nor any grief or crying or pain.
(Revelation 21:3-4)

M ost men
have
a secret desire
to make others
happy.

To give flesh to this dream
some men come
to the priesthood.
Their fervent intent
is to create joy
in the lives of others
by being
the bearers of God
and
of the good things
of God.

Many are the times
and the places
where the priest
brings the joy of God
to men:
in the pulpit
where he brings the happiness
of God's Word;
in the sacraments
where he brings God and man
fiercely together.
Indeed
just by his *living*
as a priest
he makes a joyous statement
on the value
and meaning
of life.

I bring you good news of a great joy
that is to be felt by all the people.
(Luke 2:10)

"God has given us
a memory
that we might
have roses in December,"
James Barrie once wrote.

Our memory
keeps alive the good
and true things
we experience in June,
that is,
in the beautiful times
of our lives.
It recalls
these cheering experiences
to give us strength
in the dank and difficult
Decembers
of our lives.
This is precisely why
the memory of God's people
carries forward
the easeful events
of earlier salvation history:
so that
the remembrance of them
may be a bulwark
of strength
to us
in present troubled times.

Seek Yahweh and his strength,
seek his face untiringly;
remember the marvels he has done,
his wonders, the judgments from his mouth.
(Psalm 105:4-5)

In the matter of
God's goodness
we have got to be
irrational.

This is the way it is
with love, for instance,
and with any other
deep down, visceral persuasion.
We go beyond reason,
we do not trust
appearances.
All surface indications
to the contrary
we have got to believe that
God is good,
unfailingly good to us.
Even in the thick
of troubles,
in moments of
dire tragedy,
calamity,
disaster,
God is being good.
This is illogical,
it is nonsense
but it is true.
His goodness
is never
one whit diminished,
obscured
or blunted.

Who can separate us from Christ's love?
Can trouble or misfortune or persecution or
hunger or destitution or danger or the sword? . . .
For I am convinced that neither death nor life
nor angels nor their hierarchies nor the present
nor the future nor any supernatural forces either
of height or depth nor anything else in creation
will be able to separate us from the love God
has shown in Christ Jesus our Lord!
(Romans 8:35-38)

God's love stays constant
through the thick
and thin
contingencies of life.

Even in the bleak
and trying moments
of our existence
God's love is alive
and beaming.
It is like a star:
in bright sunlight,
though invisible,
it is nonetheless there,
strongly there;
in turbulent weather,
in cloudiness and fog,
it remains fixed and
firm and shining.

The only response
that one can make
to such unfaltering love
is to say with the Psalmist:
"I look to no one else
in Heaven,
I delight in nothing else
on earth.
My heart's Rock, my own,
God for ever!"†

†Psalm 73:25-26

Can you not buy five sparrows for two pennies?
And yet not one is forgotten in God's sight.
. . . There is no need to be afraid: you are
worth more than hundreds of sparrows!
(Luke 12:6-7)

16

A man
sits in an airline terminal
for hours
feasting his eyes on those with
destinations.
What a satisfaction to have
a destination in life!
What a horror to
drift *aimlessly* through life!

Have you ever stopped to think
that Christ has delivered us from
such a pitiable condition as that—
the condition of not being able
to move effectively
toward a clear-cut goal.
Christ said: "I am the way"† and
"I am the light".*

It is by means of a path,
and light
that we can organize our movement.
By means of a path
we can successfully make our way
through the woods;
by means of light
we orient ourselves;
we can know where we are and
where we must head for.

All this is to say that
the coming of Christ into our life
endows it with a destination
and with the joyful hope of
attaining it.

†John 14:6
*John 8:12

You will reveal the path of life to me.
(Psalm 16:11)

"And they left
the presence of the council,
rejoicing that they
had been found worthy
to suffer indignity
for Jesus' name."†

No need to imagine
that the Apostles
were indulging
a sadistic tendency
in taking pleasure
out of this moment.
It is just that
they understood
profoundly:
that hardship endured for someone
is the most
brazenly incontrovertible proof
of love
for that person.
And so
they rejoiced
at having had to suffer
on account of Christ.

†Acts 5:41

Always, wherever we may be, we carry with us
in our body the death of Jesus, so that the life
of Jesus, too, may always be seen in our body.
Indeed, while we are still alive, we are consigned
to our death every day, for the sake of Jesus,
so that in our mortal flesh the life of
Jesus, too, may be openly shown.
(2 Corinthians 4:10-12)

19

I
t seems only fair
that we who have known
some joy
and peace
within our experience
of the Christian faith
should make this happiness
reach further to others.

Eat the fat and drink the sweet, and send portions
to him for whom nothing is prepared.
(Nehemiah 8:10)

20

A bridge collapsed
and some eighty people
were plunged to their deaths
in the turbulent waters below.

One of the bodies dredged up
during the grappling operations
was that of a man
still clutching a dollar bill,
a symbol
of all *that* man had yet to give,
all that he might have done
if time had not
run out for him.

It should be
one of our nagging fears
that we may die that way;
with our riches yet unspent,
with our talents, our skills
untried and unused in the service
of God and neighbor.

We should not be caught short
but give
while there is yet time to give.
Thus,
when our day comes to stand
before God
we must appear before him
with empty hands,
with our opportunities
for doing good
all exploited,
with our resources for making men happy
all depleted.

Another way of saying, perhaps,
that our Christian pilgrimage
must be one grand spending spree.

Everything will soon come to an end . . . Each
one of you has received a special grace, so, like good
stewards responsible for all these different graces
of God, put yourself at the service of others.
(1 Peter 4:7-10)

The daily papers and newscasts
make us painfully aware
of the pathos of life
on this planet.
They tell
of the little child
burned in a tenement fire,
of the elderly woman
mugged and killed
on her afternoon stroll,
of the young man
killed in a freak parkway accident.
Surely it falls
within the range of our call
to bring some relief
to this suffering.
It devolves on us
to make man's sojourn
on earth
a little less sad.

A religious observance that is pure and stainless
in the sight of God the Father is this:
to look after orphans and widows in their trouble.
(James 1:27)

How strange
that Christ should declare
fortunate,
persons who find themselves
in vile conditions of life:
poverty, starvation, persecution.

Christ seems to be saying
that these misfortunes
can be opportunities
for greatness,
for growth,
for success;
that there is a way
of viewing these conditions
as challenges,
a way of responding
that can disarm them.

Seeing the crowds, he went up the hill. There
he sat down and was joined by his disciples.
Then he began to speak.
This is what he taught them:
"How happy are the poor in spirit;
theirs is the kingdom of heaven.
Happy the gentle:
they shall have the earth for their heritage.
Happy those who mourn:
they shall be comforted.
Happy those who hunger and thirst for what is right:
they shall be satisfied.
Happy the merciful:
they shall have mercy shown them.
Happy the pure in heart:
they shall see God.
Happy the peacemakers:
they shall be called the sons of God.
Happy those who are persecuted in the cause of right:
theirs is the kingdom of heaven.
Happy are you when people abuse you and
persecute you and speak all kinds of
calumny against you on my account.
Rejoice and be glad, for your reward
will be great in heaven;
this is how they persecuted the
prophets before you."
(Matthew 5:1-12)

If, as it seems,
a person is
defined
by his relationships
to others,
it is significant that
often in Matthew's
infancy narrative,
the reference is to
"the child and his mother."
In other words,
Mary
is not designated
by name
but
by her quality as
"*His* mother."
She draws
her identity
from the *Child*.

This stands
as an *ideal* for us;
that people should
think and speak of us
in terms of *Christ*.

I am the vine, you are the branches.
Anyone who remains united to me, with me united
to him, will be very fruitful, for you cannot do
anything apart from me.
(John 15:5)

Faith
is saying "yes."

There are countless ways
of saying "yes"
each with its own gradation
of intensity.
One may speak
an impatient, reluctant
"yes"
given perhaps
out of a sense of constraint.
One can utter
a mild, minimal,
disinterested
"yes."
One can express
a merely adequate
"yes."
But one can also articulate
a full-throated, enthusiastic,
emphatic "yes."

This is the way Mary
framed her assent
to God:
with vigor,
with abandon,
lovingly.

"I am the handmaid
of the Lord,
let what you have said
be done to me."†
that is to say:
yes,
yes, with all my heart.

†Luke 1:38

Once the hand is laid on the plough, no one
who looks back is fit for the kingdom of God.
(Luke 9:62)

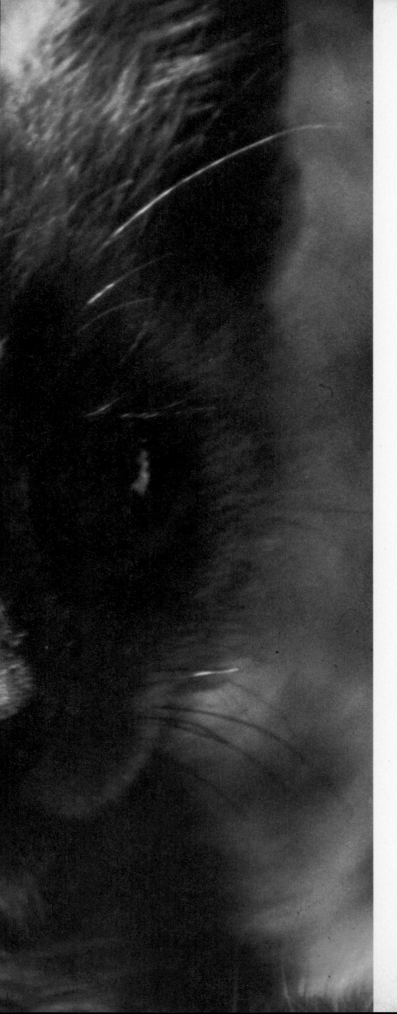

"I am with you . . .
and my spirit remains among you.
Do not be afraid!"†

In the face
of so stark
and stunning
a guarantee,
what credible reason
can you adduce
to withold your trust
in God?

†Haggai 2:4

Do not let your hearts be troubled. Trust in God
still,and trust in me.
(John 14:1)

27

"Evil is never done
so thoroughly
as when it is done
with good conscience":
a maxim of Pascal's to be
pondered with great earnestness
in these times
when we are being exhorted
as never before
to act
according to our conscience.

Is our good conscience,
however,
so poorly formed
as to constitute a menace
to the security
and happiness of
our fellowman?
Ponder this:
no matter how "good"
our conscience may be,
are there not times
when the welfare
of our neighbor
requires us to defer?

You must take care that this right of yours does
not prove a hindrance to the overscrupulous . . .
for this overscrupulous brother, for whom Christ
died, is ruined by what you call your knowledge.
But in sinning against your brothers in this way
and wounding their too scrupulous consciences,
you are really sinning against Christ. Therefore,
if what I eat makes my brother fall, I will never
eat meat again, rather than make my brother fall.
(1 Corinthians 8:9-13)

Ever since you were very young,
you have been told
that to love Christ
is a beautiful, necessary thing;
a shimmering ideal to have in life.
But how can you know
if you love Christ
and how can you know
how much you love Him?

By the excitement you feel
when His name is mentioned?
By your willingness
to endure martyrdom for Him?
Probably not.
There is a truer, if harsher
measuring rod of your affection:
the measure of your love for Christ
is the love that you have
for the person you love least.
Unhappily, this seems to be the insinuation
of Christ's own words:
"Love your enemies and pray for those
who persecute you."†
And these words must be read
against the background
of something else Christ said:
"You are my friends if you do
what I command you."*
Your readiness to obey Christ's *commands*
declares your love for Him—
and Christ has *commanded*
that you love your enemies.

Do you love Christ madly enough
to do just this?
The measure of your love for Christ
is the love that you have
for the person you love least.

†Matthew 5:44
*John 15:14

I have given you an example so that you
may copy what I have done.
(John 13:15)

Joan Marie
has gone
to God
and left a beautiful memory
behind.

The memory of
a deep devotion to Christ,
the memory of
a warm love
for family and friends,
the memory of
a remarkable openness
to life,
to music,
to nature,
to painting,
to neighbors;
to the world as
God made it
and man embellishes it.
Such was
the life of
Joan Marie,
such is
the memory
that is bequeathed
those of us
who are left behind.

Let us
hold on to that memory
with gratitude,
with affection and
with very great pride.

What will your eulogy sound like?

The memory of the righteous is a blessing.
(Proverbs 10:7)

Do something beautiful
for God:
let someone
feel the rich warmth
of your love.
You will be revealing
something of God
thereby.
God,
to be sure,
is Love
and you must not be content
merely to say so
but in your actions
you must bear
that same witness.
Actions
speak louder
than words
—this is as true
when you are trying
to bring God home
to people
as at any other time.

I have made your name known to them
and will continue to make it known.
(John 17:26)

L et us begin with
a crashing understatement.

Let us say:
things are not well with the world.
In fact,
we could say
with even greater accuracy:
things are less well with our world
than they have been in recent times.

There is drug abuse,
racial tension,
increased crime and
a whole array of
less-than-comfortable situations.
In the face of these
gross and noxious facts
we must be persuaded
that we
have something to offer
in alleviation.
We
can somehow ease
the griefs that beset our world.
We
have some answers and solutions
that derive from
the teaching of Christ.

In other words
we must be aware
that we are not
so much part of the difficulty
as we are part of
God's creative solution to it.

You are the salt of the earth! . . . You are the
light of the world! A city that is built upon a hill
cannot be hidden. People do not light a lamp
and put it under a peck-measure; they put it on
its stand and it gives light to everyone in the house.
(Matthew 5:13-15)

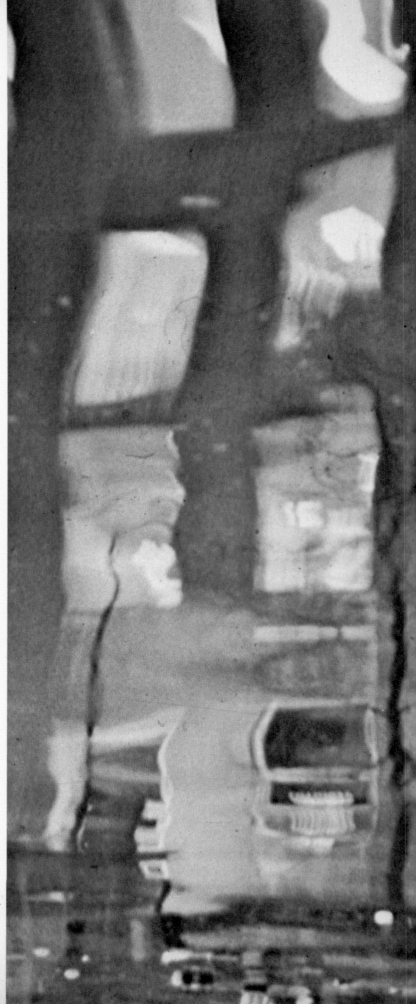

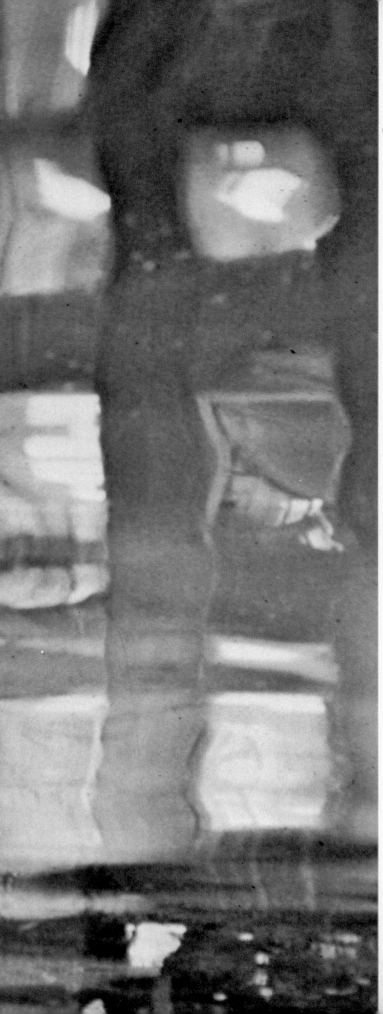

"I
have this complaint
to make;
you have
less love now
than you used to."†

That first fervor
is pitifully fragile
we probably realize
from our own
experience
but
we may not
have realized that
we bear a responsibility
for keeping it alive,
as these words
disconcertingly imply.
Has the intensity
of our love
and dedication
wound down?
Can this sad indictment
be leveled
against us
and against our congregation
as it was
once spoken
against the Ephesians?
"You have less love now
than you used to."†

†Revelations 2:4

You forget the Rock who begot you,
unmindful now of the God who fathered you.
(Deuteronomy 32:18)

More often than not
conscience is
what the *observer* invokes
rather than the doer.
It is the one who
is merely looking on
and not involved
who is prone to have
a moral sensitivity.

Pass no more judgments upon other people, so that
you may not have judgment passed upon you.
(Matthew 7:1)

———————————

"For his kindness is everlasting"

Over and over again,
for 26 times
this refrain returns
in Psalm 136.
It bears
a warm and comforting truth
about God.
One that we cannot hear
often enough.
How much bigger
would our fears and anxieties
have cause to be if
we could not say this of God:
that his kindness endures forever.

For he is gracious and merciful,
Slow to anger and abounding in kindness,
And relenting of evil.
(Joel 2:13)

It was an agonizing moment.
The enemy was in hot pursuit
and bid fair
to overtake them.
Elisha and his servant
were in bad straits.
The servant,
a young man,
was paralyzed with fear.
Elisha began to pray
in his behalf
and the boy was forthwith reassured
by a vision of horsemen and chariots
materializing
the strength of God,
now placed at their disposal.
Religious
have a role to play
that is similar to Elisha's.
By their life
and prayer
they must open the eyes of people
to spiritual reality.

I will teach you concerning the power of God;
What is with the Almighty I will not hide.
(Job 27:11)

"Bel crouches,
Nebo cowers.
They cannot
rescue the load
but themselves
go into captivity."†

Bel and Nebo
were
the chief deities
of Babylon.
But
as Isaiah
sardonically points out,
in time of trouble
the people of Babylon
had to rescue *them*
rather than the reverse,
as one would expect.

Regrettably
this is just as true
of the idols
you have
so confidently
installed in your life:
they are powerless
to save.

†Isaiah 46:1

A forgotten truth:
Mary
is an opportunity
for encountering Christ.

Our forefathers
seemed to have understood this
well
and to have expressed it
in allusions
of rare charm.
This is surely
what they sought to say
when they spoke
of Mary as
"House of Gold",
"Ark of the Covenant",
"Gateway of the Great King".
They conceived of Mary
as the precious
container
that drew
its meaning and beauty
from the precious One
contained,
Christ.

Mary
is a "place"
for meeting
Christ.

There is no salvation through anyone else,
for there is no one else in the world who has been
named to men as our only means of being saved.
(Acts 4:12)

The holy Spirit will come over you, and the power
of the Most High will overshadow you. For that reason
your child will be called holy, and the Son of God.
(Luke 1:35)

One of the most dangerous pretexts
that man can make use of
is the word
tomorrow.
Tomorrow bespeaks postponement.
Christ warns against
the mistake of putting off
till tomorrow
what must be done today;
especially
in the matter of salvation
and the life of the spirit.

These are the *urgencies*
of the present,
not the *task*
of the future.
This is what Christ means
when he says:
"Let your loins be girded
and your lamps burning.
Be like men
who are waiting
for the Master to come home."†
There is a ferocious emphasis
on the *now* in these words.

Bear in mind that
"Yesterday is but a dream
and tomorrow
is only a vision,
but today well-lived
makes every tomorrow
a vision of hope!
Look well therefore to this day."*

†Luke 12:35
*Salutation of the Dawn

Night is coming, when no one can do any work.
(John 9:4)

36

'Is that all there is;
is that all there is?"
Plaintive words
from a song that reviews
a series of recollections
of an unhappy and frustrated past.

Are you ever moved
to ask this question
as it concerns your experience
in the Christian faith:
"Is that *all* there is?"
Have I tasted all the joys
and all the comforts
of Christian commitment?

The answer is a resounding *no*.

No because the Christian experience
is an adventure toward God,
and we have not yet arrived.

No because, as the philosophers say,
God is always greater and larger
than you have ever succeeded
in realizing Him.
There is more to God
than any of us can experience
of Him in our lifetime.

At most, we have perhaps
"touched the hem of
His garment."
Undreamed of satisfactions
await us
as we make our way toward God.

Things which no eye ever saw and no ear
ever heard, and never occurred to the human mind,
which God has provided for those who love him.
(1 Corinthians 2:9)

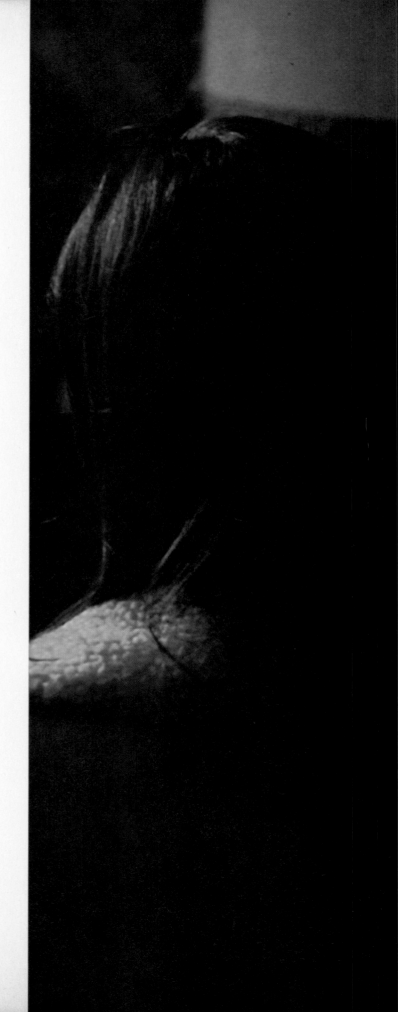

"The joy of the Lord
is your refuge"†

The comfort
and serene assurance
of this word
must be carried to our youth
in their loneliness and alienation;
to the middle-aged,
tortured by a creeping sense of mediocrity;
to the aged,
laboring under a sense of rejection;
to every man
who broods over a wound.

†Nehemiah 8:10

So you, too, are sorrowful now; but I will see you
again, and your hearts will be happy, and no one
can rob you of your happiness.
(John 16:22)

"Memory is like a crazy woman
who hoards colored rags
and throws away food."

A foolish way to relate to the past.

What do you remember
of your early experiences
in the Catholic Faith?

Is it a misunderstanding
you once had with a priest?
Is it an unfortunate episode
you had in a Catholic school?
Are these the only memories
of your Catholic past
that you can muster?
What good does it do
to hold onto
only the unpleasant images
of the past?

Have you forgotten
those moments of peace and relief
that you have known many times
after a good confession?
Have you lost sight of
the satisfactions in prayer
that God has often
granted to you in the past?
Some people seem
constitutionally unable
to recall anything but
their less happy moments
of life in the Church.

This is warped,
as the woman was warped
who hoarded the colored rags
and threw away the food.

Then I remembered your mercy, Lord,
and your deeds from earliest times.
(Ecclesiasticus 51:8-11)

There are three kinds
of persons
who come and
volunteer to Christ.

The first prays:
"I am a bow in your hands,
O Lord,
draw me lest I rot."

The second prays:
"Do not overdraw me,
Lord,
I shall break."

The third prays:
"Overdraw me,
Lord, and
who cares if I break?"

Which one of these are you?

But the souls of the upright are in the hand of God.
(Wisdom 3:1)

The Gospel of Matthew
begins with
a listing of some
of Christ's
earthly forebears.
These were the persons
who helped make
the coming of Christ
possible.

In a sense
you too
are part of the genealogy
of Christ
because you too
in your own way
make the coming of Christ
possible.
Just as
He once came to Palestine
you
make Him come
into the world
in which you live and work.

There was a crowd sitting around him when they
told him, "Your mother and your brothers are
outside asking for you."
He answered, "Who are my mother and my brothers?"
And looking around at the people sitting about
him, he said, "Here are my mother and my brothers!
Whoever does the will of God is my brother
and sister and mother."
(Mark 3:32-35)

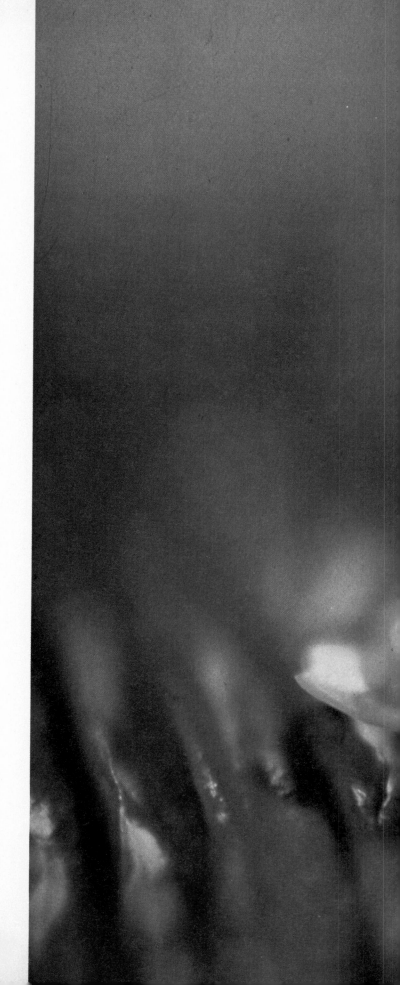

Once, when the Israelites
tired of
the blazing spirituality of God,
they sought
to represent him
in a material way.
More than likely
that is what
the statue of the golden calf portrayed;
not an alien god but
Yahweh himself
in material form.

Are we,
in the same way,
trying to experience God
on our own terms?
Are we tired of
his cool transcendence?
Do we want a
more *manageable* God?
One
more easily
and
more satisfyingly
encountered?

In short,
a more understandable God,
one that falls wholly
within the compass of
our experience
as bulls and calves did
within the experience
of the ancient Israelites?

Therefore, stand in awe of the Lord, and serve him
faithfully and loyally . . . However, if you find it
obnoxious to serve the Lord, choose today whom you
will serve . . . as for me and my house, we will serve
the Lord.
(Joshua 24:14-15)

There is
a certain attractiveness
to the *mystery* of God.
It suggests a depth of being
that no man's mind can reach,
an elusive beauty
that largely escapes man's clutch.
This is something
to revel in
rather than
to apologize for
because, paradoxically,
by its very silence,
the mystery of God
communicates something valid
about him:
a deep shadow can be cast
only by a strong light.
God remains untamed
by man's logic,
unpackaged by his rhetoric.
The full dimensions
of God
must remain forever inconceivable
to man,
unguessed at by him.

How inexhaustible God's resources, wisdom, and
knowledge are! How unfathomable his decisions are,
and how untraceable his ways!
(Romans 11:33)

When Christ comes to the disciples
walking on the water,
they first see a vague form
whom they do not recognize.
It is only
when they look again,
more carefully,
that they make out
the form of Christ.
We too must
look again at our neighbor,
and when we do
we will see
not a vague person
but Christ.

Toward morning he went out to them, walking on
the sea. And the disciples saw him walking on the sea,
and they were terrified and said, "It is a ghost!"
And they screamed with fear. But Jesus immediately
spoke to them and said, "Take courage! It is I."
(Matthew 14:25-27)

47

One
of the carefully
nurtured hopes
of the Christian apostolate
is to set such an example
of good life and action
as to turn people's minds
to God.
To promote the deduction:
he is so good;
how *good*
must his God be.

Your light must shine in the sight of men,
so that, seeing your good works, they may give
the praise to your Father in heaven.
(Matthew 5:16)

There is a power in smallness.

The mere 26 letters
of the alphabet
can be combined and juggled
into words and sentences
that carry the deepest thoughts
of one man to another.
The scant 10 digits
on a telephone dial
can be used to
put two individuals into dialogue
across the distance
of a continent or an ocean.

The fact
of smallness
therefore
must not automatically be taken
to be incapacitating.
Realize that
even if your group of workers,
your circle of friends
or your religious associates
have dwindled drastically in numbers,
few as they may now be,
they can be taken up
by the Holy Spirit
and used as His triumphant vehicle.

For,
God works
in wondrous ways
His marvels to achieve.

Do not be afraid, little flock, for your Father
has chosen to give you the kingdom.
(Luke 12:32)

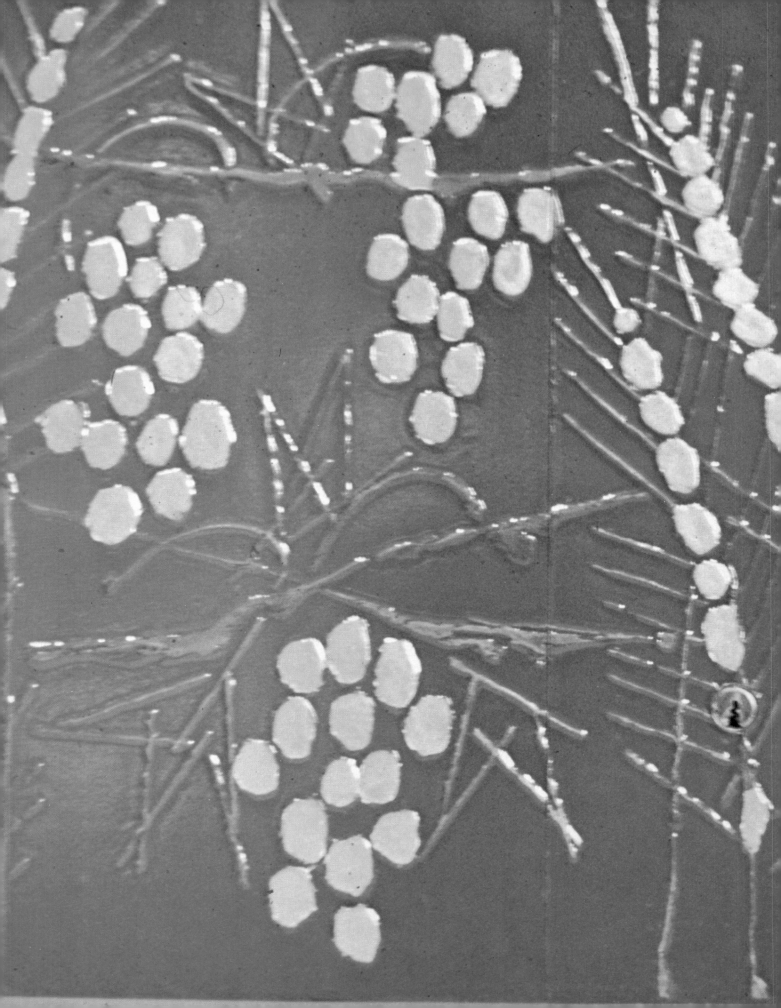

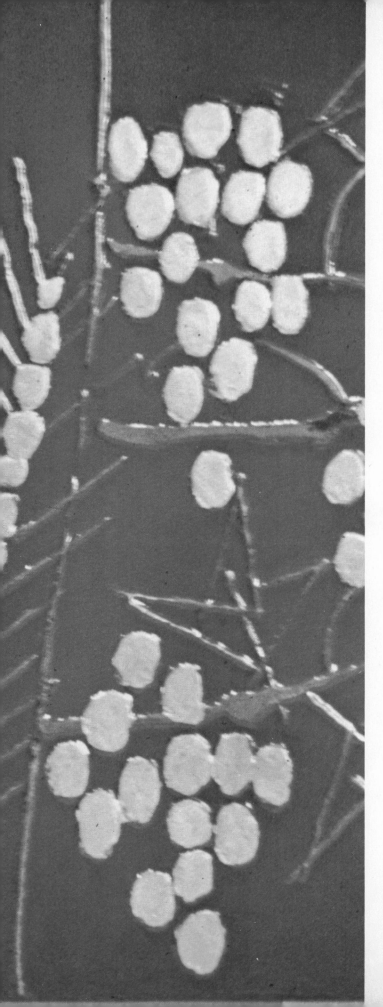

"I feel sorry
for all these people:
they have been with me
for three days now
and have nothing to eat.
I do not want
to send them off hungry,
they might collapse on the way."†

These words
are charged with compassion
and graciousness.
And you must know
that the compassion of Christ
has not diminished
with the passage of time.
Christ is still concerned
to provide for people's needs,
for your needs,
to give you some joy and comfort
as you pilgrimage through life.
That is why
He grants *you*
the Eucharist.

Each time the Eucharist
is made present,
it is with *you* in mind.
It is as if Christ
were saying once again,
"I do not want
to send them off hungry,
they might collapse
on the way."†

†Matthew 15:32

Your love, Yahweh, reaches to the heavens,
your faithfulness to the clouds.
(Psalm 36:5)

How many
are the ways that
you can enrich another man's
existence.
You can introduce him
to the warmth of human love,
to the pleasures of good food,
to the delight of
exciting ideas
and above all
to the strength and serenity
of God's truth.

The Scripture says: Not on bread alone is man to live,
but on every word that comes from the mouth of God!
(Matthew 4:4)

We live
too comfortably
with the naive notion
that we
come to God
strictly by
our own choice.
We blithely speak of
"asking to be baptized",
or "entering religious life",
as though
these steps
are taken solely
and primarily
at our discretion.
We are
seemingly oblivious
of the fact
that it is God
who takes the initiative
in these
and in every instance
of drawing near.
He
always makes
the first move.

"It was not you
who chose Me,
it is I
who have chosen you."†
A humbling thought
perhaps
but an altogether
satisfying one.

†John 15:16

The Lord said to Abram, "Leave your land, your relatives, and your father's home, for the land that I will show you; and I will make a great nation of you." (Genesis 12:1-2)

In the 6th. Century A.D.
an Egyptian cartographer attempted
to fashion a map of the world
in the form of a rectangle
with Jerusalem
at the center.

This was a quaint,
yet sincere,
attempt to express
a fundamental Christian conviction;
that the events
which transpired in Jerusalem:
the Passion,
Death and
Resurrection
of Christ
are at the *center*
of history and life;
they are at the
very center
of our lives.

You are built upon the apostles and prophets as
your foundation, and Christ Jesus himself is the
cornerstone. Through him every part of the building
is closely united and grows into a temple sacred
through its relation to the Lord.
(Ephesians 2:20-21)

Good Friday—Holy Saturday
the one only day
in Christian memory
that records
a dead Christ.

But
from that day
until this,
He
has been *alive*
and *well*
and *active*
in the lives of Christians.

I will *always* be with you, to the very close of the age.
(Matthew 28:20)

To work for fulfillment
in religious life
is much like trying
to catch up to one's own shadow;
each step towards it
makes it recede
by just that much.
Fulfillment
must come
as God's free gift.
It cannot be earned,
programmed,
demanded.

Because you . . . have not asked for yourself long
life nor riches nor the life of your enemies, but have
asked for yourself understanding to perceive
justice; behold, I have done according to your word
. . . I give also what you did not ask, both riches
and honor, so that, all your days, there shall not be
any like you among the kings.
(1 Kings 3:11-13)

The objectives of religious life
can be framed in the simplest terms:
to achieve
a heightened awareness
of the divine mysteries
that lie beyond
human experience,
to acknowledge
the truth and grandeur
of these mysteries
in prayer,
and to chart a personal life
that sharply accords
with these mysteries
or, as Micah put it:
"To do justly,
to love mercy
and to walk humbly
with Thy God."

Yahweh, who has the right to enter your tent, or to
live on your holy mountain? The man whose way
of life is blameless, who always does what is right,
who speaks the truth from his heart.
(Psalm 15:1-2)

H ow very rich
with meanings
is the phenomenon of Christ.
Perhaps the most basic is
Christ's indispensability.
Christ
is desperately needed
to give substance
to man's optimism.

Man's great hopes
for himself,
for the world,
his bright dreams,
would lift and dry up
like the morning dew
if Christ were not here
to give possibility to them.
Without Christ
there would be no chance at all
for penetrating
the ambiguities of life
and deciphering its meaning.
Without Christ
there is no meaning to life,
there is just a booming emptiness.

. . . the Lion of the tribe of Judah, the Root of David,
has triumphed, and he will open the scroll and
the seven seals of it. Then I saw, standing between
the throne . . . a Lamb that seemed to have
been sacrificed. . . . Then I saw the Lamb
break one of the seven seals.
(Revelation 5:5-6:1)

59

Devotion to the Saints is
a fading value among us.
It has become
badly declassé.
For it seems to many
so terribly naive in this age
of theological sophistication
to turn to persons who,
when they lived on earth,
more often than not passed for
mere peasants or simple folk.
What can such people
contribute
to us?

They can lead us to God!

For all their littleness,
or perhaps,
because of it,
they can speak to us of God
with very great impact.
Perhaps,
we have dismissed the Saints
too hastily
from our faith experience.
Perhaps we believe
they are beneath our notice;
they are unhelpful to *modern* man.

And yet,
they may be saying
to us
the very things
we have to hear.

Let the children come to me and do not try to stop
them, for the Kingdom of God belongs to such
as they. I tell you whoever does not accept the
Kingdom of God like a child will not enter it at all.
(Luke 18:16-17)

To be great
is to be
misunderstood.
Regrettably,
this seems
to be as true
in our faith commitment
as it is
generally
in life.

For we have become a spectacle to the whole
universe, angels as well as men. We are made fools of,
for the sake of Christ.
(1 Corinthians 4:9)

_____

The easy circumstances
of life
riches
fame
abundance
can prove to be the undoing of a person,
occasions of failure;
the repeating
in one's own existence
of the parable of Lazarus
and the rich man.

It is easier for a camel to get through a needle's eye
than for a rich man to get into the Kingdom of God!
(Matthew 19:24)

Mighty Jerusalem
missed the opportunity
of its life:
the opportunity
of *all eternity*.
This is the same tragedy
that too often
befalls men today:
they let slip through their hands
the chance
to lay hold of *something*
of God.

You do not know either me or my Father. If you
knew me, you would know my Father too.
(John 8:19)

————————————

For years on end
Jesus lived in Nazareth
in obscurity
as he grew
and quietly prepared
for his great work.
Every Christian
must have
a Nazareth
in his life:
a place, a time
for growing
in shadow and silence.

And he went back with them to Nazareth
and obeyed them.
(Luke 2:51)

On one occasion
Jesus
censured his contemporaries
in these terms:
"We played the pipes
for you
and you wouldn't dance.
We sang dirges,
and
you wouldn't cry."†

These words
are an indictment
of the insensitivity
of some people
to God's truth
and purposes.
They speak
of a frivolous rejection
of God's overtures
to men.

If Christ Himself
encountered such indifference
as He went about
preaching the Good News
why should we be
unsettled
when we, in our turn,
meet up with
similar unresponsiveness
in our attempts
to bring God
and His truth
to men?

†Luke 7:32

The disciple is not superior to his teacher,
nor the slave to his master. . . . If they have
called the master of the house Beelzebul,
what will they not say of his household?
(Matthew 10:24-25)

"Let not thy learning
exceed thy deeds.
Mere knowledge is not the goal
but action."

Wise words
taken from the Talmud
saying something that is
strong and necessary for us.

How laughable
some persons in our midst
make themselves by talking
so glibly of love
and being so obviously
unloving.
Think of
their expressed attitudes
toward established authority;
too often
gratuitously hostile.

How incredible
they make themselves
by their incessant chatter
about community
while being so intolerant
of differing tastes and personalities.

We must learn from their failures.

Let it not be said
of us
as, I believe,
it can be said
of them:
vox, vox et praeterea nihil:
words, words and nothing else.

Do people
still complain
of not being made
to hear God's truth?
If they do,
it is probably
not because
it has never been proposed
to them
but rather because
it has been spoken to them
woodenly,
perfunctorily perhaps,
and not
with the vigor,
care and passion
that it demands.

My brothers, what is the good of a man's saying he has
faith, if he has no good deeds to show?
(James 2:14)

What I tell you in the dark you must say in the light,
and what you hear whispered in your ear,
you must proclaim from the housetops.
(Matthew 10:27)

"He is
never far
from any of us."†
A reassuring truth
that takes
the edge of strangeness
off life.
No place is desolate
or remote;
for wherever it may lie,
it cannot close out
the presence of God.
"He is
never far
from any of us."

No situation
in life
can be really desperate
because no situation
can negate this fact:
"He is never far
from any
of us."
What is there then
that can blight
our Christian hope;
for apparently
there is no person,
place or thing
that can neutralize
the exhilarating truth
that God is
never far from
any of us.

†Acts 17:27

Even as the mountains encircle Jerusalem,
So the Lord encircles his people,
Henceforth and forever.
(Psalm 125:2)

65

E very man
ought to be thought of
as a new experiment
in God's laboratory.
This is
just another way of saying
that God is aware
of each one of us
as individuals
with all our exciting
distinctiveness
and not as mere blurs
in the vast crowd
of humanity.

Surely
this was the way
Christ related to people
during His time on earth.
When he was asked
to heal the man who
was deaf and dumb
he did not content himself
to effect the cure
by a mere flick of His will;
as it were,
with detachment.
Instead
he insisted on
the *personal* touch.
He put his fingers
into the man's ears
and touched his tongue.

The life I now live in this body I live in faith:
faith in the Son of God who loved *me* and who
sacrificed himself for *my* sake.
(Galations 2:20)

66

This seems
to be the law
of Christ's coming—
it follows upon
suffering.

In Palestine
John the Baptist
had first
to come
and be arrested
before
Christ came
announcing
the good news.

In our world
it may be just so.
We may have to prepare
His way
by our suffering.

We struggle,
we suffer
here in the vineyard
and then
Christ comes.

God give us the strength.

After John was arrested, Jesus went into Galilee
proclaiming the good news from God.
(Mark 1:14)

It was only
after Christ's suffering
and death,
after the Apostles'
anguished experience
of persecution
that Christian communities
began to sprout up
and to thrive.
Is this then
the law of Christian communities:
they are born out of pain,
they develop
out of suffering?

Did not the Christ have to suffer thus before
entering upon his glory?
(Luke 24:26)

There is a story in the Southwest
of a series of Franciscan friars
who came to evangelize a pueblo
in what is now New Mexico.
As the first ones arrived,
and before they could
so much as explain their mission,
they were promptly put to death
by the unfriendly and suspicious Indians.
But more kept coming,
to the number of nine.
This set the Indians thinking
that there must be
some rugged, driving force
that compelled these men
to come to them.
Finally when the *tenth* man came
they heard him out
and embraced the Faith.

How many times
have *we* come to our assignments
as the tenth priest came to the Indians?
We too have appeared
on a scene that *others*
had prepared before us
and given their lives to.
We too have reaped harvests
that other men have planted.
It was *others*
who opened doors for us,
it was they who gained
respectful hearings for us.

Richly have we received
from the past,
richly must *we*
donate to the future.

I did the planting, Apollos the watering, but
it was God who made the plants grow. ... The
planter and the waterer are all one, though
each of us will be paid for his own work.
For we are fellow-laborers for God.
(1 Corinthians 3:6-9)

70

Once there lived a young man
of brilliant mind
and noble spirit
who cherished one, single desire:
to know the secret of
achievement and success
in human life.

For years he
pondered and prayed over this
until one night,
in a dream,
a hoary old sage came to him
bearing the answer to the secret.
He said,
simply,
"Stretch out your hand and
reach what you can."
But the young man,
gravely disappointed, said:
"No, it cannot be that,
it must be
something harder; something
more satisfying to the human spirit."

The old man replied softly,
"You are right, it is something
harder. It is this:
Stretch out your hand and
reach *what you cannot!*"

The Christian soul is like that.
It goes through life
stretching out its hand for
what is beyond its reach. It
dreams of living beyond death,
it dreams of living happy
forever, it dreams of
possessing God.

But
humanly speaking
all this would be impossible;
but then comes Christ
and makes the impossible, possible.

He says,
"I have come that you
may have life, and may have it
more abundantly.† I am
the Resurrection
and the Life.* I am
the way to God."°

†John 10:10
*John 11:25
°John 14:6

For I tell you, if you have faith the size of a grain
of mustard, you can say to this mountain,
"Move from here over to there!" and it will move,
and nothing will be impossible for you.
(Matthew 17:20)

72

One of the touching legends
that sprang up around
the holy memory of
St. Francis of Assisi
tells how one day
the saint walked up to an almond tree
and said:
Sister, speak to me of God;
and the almond tree *blossomed.*

This story in its way
defines the best hopes
of every Christian,
for we have all heard
the world address
the same demand to us:
sometimes shamefacedly,
sometimes bluntly, sometimes subtly
but *always* insistently,
the world keeps saying:
speak to me of God,
do for me as Christ would.

This then should be
our deeply cherished hope:
that we may respond
as beautifully, as dramatically,
as did the almond tree.
That is to say, we must
project our life
as a pursuit of excellence
so that the sheer strength and
beauty of our life and work,
our achievements,
our thought and speech
will speak loudly and clearly
to the world *of God.*

How happy is the man who has not walked in the
counsel of the wicked . . . For he is like a tree planted
by streams of water, that yields its fruit in its season.
(Psalm 1:1-3)

75

"Ephphatha—be thou opened."†

A man is largely deaf
to the beauty
and rhythms
of life,
its inner meanings,
until Christ
enters into him as
Christ entered
into the existence of
the deaf man in the Gospel
and opened his ears
that he might hear.

†Mark 7:31

To you has been intrusted the secret of the reign
of God, but to those outsiders, everything
is offered in figures, so that
"They may look and look and yet not see,
And listen and listen and yet not understand."
(Mark 4:11-12)

Once . . .
a man
had a curious dream.

He saw himself
already dead,
and in his amazement
he cried out,
"I can't be dead,
I haven't lived yet!"

That cry was
really a protest;
an outcry against
the emptiness of his life.
Nothing had happened
there yet
to make *that* life significant.

This must not
be so
in our lives.
If we put God *there*
God is large enough to occupy
the vast spaces of human life;
to fill the wide expanse
of human aspiration.

If you
were to have this dream
tonight
would you have to say:
"I haven't lived yet", or
could you better say:
"Dismiss your servant in peace
oh Lord,
for my eyes have seen
your salvation"?†

†Luke 2:29

Yahweh, you yourself are my lamp,
my God lights up my darkness.
(Psalm 18:28)

"Let the waste land
rejoice and bloom;
let it bring forth flowers
like the jonquil.
Then the eyes of the blind
shall be opened,
the ears of the deaf unsealed,
the lame shall leap like deer,
water
gushes in the desert,
streams
in the waste land,
the scorched earth becomes a lake,
the parched land
springs of water."†

All these prodigies are
in themselves impossible
or at least most difficult to achieve
but
under the touch of God
they come to pass.
So, in our own lives
God can make
the impossible happen.
Are you
firmly persuaded of this?
Remember:
"Everything is possible
with God";*
"There is nothing I cannot master
with the help of the One
who gives me strength."°

†Isaiah 35:1-7
*Mark 10:27
°Phillippians 4:13

Go back and tell John what you hear and see;
the blind see again and the lame walk,
lepers are cleansed and the deaf hear, and
the dead are raised to life and the Good News
is proclaimed to the poor.
(Matthew 11:4-5)

To meet God,
Jacob stood alone.

After having put aside
everything and everyone
who might distract from
his experience of God
Jacob stood grandly alone.

There are times
when every Christian
must feel the need
of doing the same;
of going away to a quiet place,
to stand alone and
strongly experience God.

He took them, and sent them across the stream,
and sent everything that belonged to him across.
Jacob himself was left behind all alone.
(Genesis 32:23-24)

80

Would it be too shocking to say
that Christ's birth
must be our death?
Yet
in a sense
that is true.

When Christ is born
in our lives
we must somehow die.
We must die
to those misshapen values
we once lived by.
We must die
to the prejudices
that once governed our lives.
We must die
to the callousness
we once harbored
toward our neighbor's
hurts and needs.
We must die
in these little ways
so that we may live
unto Christ
in a large way.

What else
can our Lord have meant
when he said:
"Whoever wants
to preserve his own life
will lose it
and whoever loses his life
for Me
will find it."†

†Matthew 16:25

I tell you, unless a grain of wheat falls on the
ground and dies, it remains just one grain.
But if it dies, it yields a great harvest.
(John 12:24)

A man fears death because he fears the unknown. All that a man can know is life. And death, it appears to him, is the opposite of life and as such remains dark and impenetrable. And so man shrinks from it in horror

as from a fearful
and obscene thing.

But this is to be
oblivious
of the fact
that Christ has come

and said:
"I am the Resurrection
and the Life."†

Several *other* things
Christ has said
about death
—all couched
in terms of life,
that same strong,
colorful
life
that one experiences
here on this planet.
He spoke
about death
in terms of life,
a terminology we can
easily fathom.
He has given us
to understand
that death
is not the finish
of life.
It is
the first *split second*
of a new
and brighter life.

"In Death,
Life is not
taken away,
but only changed."*

†John 11:25
*From Preface to the Mass

We shall all be changed, in a moment, in the
twinkling of an eye . . . Death has been
triumphantly destroyed. Where, Death, is your
victory? Where, Death, is your sting?
(1 Corinthians 15:52-55)

Christ seems always
to have attracted people
with a reckless streak in them.

Zacchaeus
who climbed a tree
like a curious little boy
to catch a glimpse of Christ
not thinking of
the foolish image he was projecting;
Nicodemus
who put
his position and prestige in jeopardy by
coming to consult Christ;
the Apostles who
gave up their trade and
comfortable way of life
to be with Christ.

Take careful note of this,
that everyone of these men
was well rewarded for his gamble.

There must surely be times when
your decision
to follow Christ
appears to you
as brash and costly.
Then is the time
to think of
Nicodemus, Zacchaeus, Peter
and the rest.
They too made a decision
that was risky,
yes,
but supereminently right and rich.

Peter started to say to him, "Well, we have left all
we had, and have followed you." Jesus said, "I tell you,
there is no one who has given up home or brothers
or sisters or mother or father or children or land for
me and for the good news, but will receive now
in this life a hundred times as much."
(Mark 10:28-29)

Suppose for the moment
that a colleague
and close friend of yours
has just brought off
a spectacular accomplishment.
Now you find yourself
in his company
but though you are aware
of his achievement
and he knows you are aware,
still you take no note of it,
not so much as
a syllable of congratulation
crosses your lips.
You preserve an awkward
silence.
This is unnatural.

Are you guilty of
such unexplainable reticence
with respect to God?
Day in, day out,
never so much
as one prayer of praise
escapes you
that would take cognizance of
God's triumphant lordship
over life and the universe.

Make a joyous shout to God, all the earth;
Praise the glory of his name;
Make his praise glorious!
(Psalm 66:1-2)

O ur trials
can be made into our greatest assets.
Our privileges
can turn out to be our worst enemies.

But when the young man heard that, he went
away much cast down, for he had
a great deal of property.
(Matthew 19:22)

———————————

"T rue instruction
was in his mouth
and no wrong
was upon his lips.
In peace
and uprightness
he walked with me,
and many
did he turn
from guilt."†

Could your life and work
for Christ
be characterized in this way?

†Malachi 2:6

Therefore, stand in awe of the Lord, and serve him
faithfully and loyally . . . However, if you find it
obnoxious to serve the Lord, choose today whom you
will serve . . . as for me and my house, we will serve
the Lord.
(Joshua 24:14-15)

"B ut my life
does not matter,
if I can only
finish my race
and do the service
entrusted to me
by the Lord Jesus,
of declaring
the good news
of God's favor."†

This is
the sort of headlong abandon
with which
you must commit yourself
to the work of the Gospel.

†Acts 20:24

———————————

D oing the work of God
among men
is sometimes like skywriting
with one's life.
One
writes the message
large
but one
does not clearly see
what one has achieved
or whether
anyone has taken notice,
much less understood.

I charge you in the sight of God and Christ Jesus
. . . preach the message; be at it in season and
out of season.
(2 Timothy 4:1-2)

Dial-a-Prayer,
it appears
is the most popular form
of recorded phone message
across the nation,
after the time
and weather.
An astonishing statistic
that seems
to be attesting to
a nostalgia for God
that some people
inexplicably
are too ashamed
to own up to
except in private,
on the telephone,
with a taped prayer.

When a man decides
to work with the blind
he is taken aside
and given a very curious directive.
He is told:
you must, yourself, become blind,
at least for a time.
With that he is sent off to a training center
where he assumes a blindfold
tightly fitted over his eyes.

For a week or so
he does not look upon the light of day.
He must grope his way around,
collecting bruises
from unsuspected pieces of furniture.
He must learn to depend on a cane
and on a sharpened sense
of smell and hearing.
Only then may that man come forward
to serve the blind.
For he has lived in their world,
he has run their risks, felt their anxieties,
now knows what it is to be blind.

Christ can quite correctly be defined
in just this fashion:
He is God who has come down
to live our life,
to see it from the inside.
And, when Christ ascended
to the Father
He took with Him
a first-hand knowledge
of what it is like to live and suffer
as a human being on this earth.
Now He does not have to imagine
what it is like to live as you live,
He has only to remember.

M an
is God's
most precious thought.
This is one of
the truths
the sacraments disclose to us.
Just as
in the human community
signs are used by men
to manifest their thoughts
and intentions
toward one another,
so God
uses these signs
to put
beyond doubt
his affection for us.
No need to wonder
or fear
what God thinks of us,
he declares himself
through the sacraments.

It was you who created my inmost self,
and put me together in my mother's womb;
for all these mysteries I thank you.
(Psalm 139:13-14)

Too often these days
we encounter within the Church
a bizarre situation:
a massive expenditure of effort
in the sacred names
of honesty and openness
just to say
or do
something negative,
or worse yet,
destructive.

It all seems silly,
comical even,
and worst of all,
unworthy of the human spirit
which is
always better employed
in building up
than in
tearing down.

And I told them how the kindly favour of God
had been with me, and also repeated the words
the king had said to me. "Let us start!"
they exclaimed, "Let us *build!*"; and with willing
hands they set about the good work.
(Nehemiah 2:18)

The Gospel presents us
with a spate of persons
who longed for Christ.
Indeed the Gospel begins
with a reference to two such persons:
Simeon and Anna, the prophetess.
They prayed and fasted
as they awaited the salvation of Israel,
that is,
the Christ.
Then there was the group of Greeks
who came up to
one of the Apostles and said:
"Sir, we should like to see the Master."

Elsewhere in the Gospel
we meet two more:
Nathanael and Philip
who were instructed by the law
and the prophets
to wait for the Messiah, the Christ.
We must not forget
that each of these persons
had his craving for Christ slaked.

That prompts us to ask ourselves:
are we living
in expectation of Christ?
To be sure
we have long since
met up with him
but do we have the hope
of drawing closer to him?

Perhaps the *main* reason
we have not achieved
greater intimacy with Christ
is simply that
we have not dared to *desire* it.

God, you are my God, I am seeking you,
my soul is thirsting for you.
(Psalm 63:1)

90

Among the ruins of Pompei
there are markings on a wall
of what was once a tavern.
These jottings show the credit
extended to customers.

All accounts are marked paid
except one —
a debt that will be forever unpaid.
For one day
with staggering suddenness
Vesuvius erupted,
the lava flowed
and all in Pompeii
was frozen at its particular stage
of accomplishment
or non-accomplishment.

We have debts
of kindness
to be paid to our fellowman,
and we
must not miss the chance
to meet these debts now
while we are able;
for the danger is that
these obligations
will be unfulfilled:
debts
forever outstanding
against us.

But you may be sure of this, that if the master of
the house had known in what part of the night
the thief was coming, he would have been
on the watch, and would not have let his house
be broken into. Therefore you must be ready too,
for the Son of Man is coming at a time
when you do not expect him.
(Matthew 24:43-44)

Today
is a day
of brilliant sunshine.

Will you
at any moment
during this day
stop to recognize
this fact?

Very probably not.

You have taken it all
for granted;
just as you may be
taking for granted
the sharp, clear
light of Christ
that is shining
in your life.

The need
is to realize
a basic fact of
our Christian life:
that our lives are warmed
and lighted
by Christ.

The city does not need the sun nor the
moon to shine in it, for the glory of God
lighted it, and the Lamb is its lamp.
(Revelation 21:23)

Guide for group expression

General Comment: This book can be used for group prayer meetings as well as for discussion groups and information classes. While this is an ideal meditation book to have in one's own library for ready reference, it can be even more important in your faith-life when shared with others at meetings and in Liturgical celebrations.

The entire tone of this book is one of positive approach. It is a series of reflections that should lead to prayer. Size of groups can vary but with large groups there should be plans for separating into smaller numbers for closer dialogue or prayer.

Each situation naturally calls for special planning. Thus the following are only guides to help leaders. Individuals will have to determine whether particular groups should spend most time with prayer, discussion, research or a form of action.

Meetings

For a *first* meeting, distribute a copy of REFLECTIONS to each person and outline a plan for a series of meetings. Briefly take the people through the book to point out the visual-theology found in the full color photography, stress the simplicity of the meditations and the desire to proceed slowly with each in order to savor the deeper meanings to be found in each person's interpretation of the thoughts.

Assign reading to be done during the week between meetings, keeping in mind that too heavy an assignment might discourage people. Suggestion: pick two or three readings with underlying similarity of theme. Each person should be asked to read a section from the Bible relative to the theme—as a start, point out the scriptural references with the meditations.

All members should be encouraged to make marginal notes in their books for the discussions and each should bring a Bible to the meetings for reference or participation in readings.

Set the tone of all meetings by opening and closing your first meeting with prayer. Use a meditation each time as a reading (or a scriptural reference) and then add a simple prayer such as the Our Father, or, with certain groups, members may formulate prayers that can be used.

SUGGESTIONS FOR GROUP DISCUSSION/INFORMATION

3 Suggested Meeting Formats
Format #1
Open meeting with reading of one of the assigned reflections and a scriptural passage. Follow this with a brief period of silence for prayer and thought.

Leader should point out connection between reading assignment and scripture used. Following this general opening, meeting should be divided into small groups of 5 or 6 people for discussion of one of the reflections that has been assigned. Leader designates which reflection will be discussed by the groups. Allow approximately 10 minutes for the discussion of this one reflection and the agreement on a mutual viewpoint as a group.

Bring all together into one large group again. Have each group leader give the impression most prevalent in each group and have each leader end his report with any questions the group might have. These questions should be taken down by an assistant leader for later discussion. After all groups have reported and raised their questions, the leader should answer as many questions as possible and make a general summation of the various reports heard. Leaders could also ask for comments from audience.

This general session portion should take about 20 to 30 minutes depending again on the nature of the assembled group and their desire for shorter or longer sessions. (At this time there could be a refreshment break during which informal answers and comments would be invited.) After break, groups re-form to discuss one of the scripture passages in light of their reading during the week and the comments just heard at the general session. At this portion leaders or clergy should move about from group to group to join in their talks, aid in direction and add some pertinent comment that will lead the group to in-depth probing. Allow a good thirty minutes for this period and again bring all together for a final general session for that meeting.

Leaders should address the group, offer general thoughts on what various summations should probably be and then invite groups or individuals to express themselves relative to what their real conclusions were versus the "accepted" conclusion. (In fact, to stimulate debate at this point, a leader could give a conclusion that would open people to debate.)

The reading assignments and any special projects should be given at this point; i.e.: search out newspapers or magazines to develop a particular theme or observation; tally up observations locally of people who really brought Christian action to a problem or a group. Formation of prayer groups using REFLECTIONS could also be undertaken after the first or second meeting if people reacted positively to the suggestion. Christian action on a particular local problem could be suggested and developed if approved by the group.

Close meeting with readings, prayers or a Liturgical or para-liturgical celebration.

Format #2

Leader opens the meeting with reading of one passage from REFLECTIONS.

Comment is invited on this one passage and what it means in the present life-style of the group. (The reading would be from one of those assigned to be read prior to meeting.) Response should be more of the impersonal, group type rather than personal comment; i.e.: "the meditation on how good God is to us made me think of how little the people of our town realize this good gift and our responsibility to do more about it."

Prepare for a Liturgical celebration using passages from REFLECTIONS as well as from Scripture. Where practical a complete service or Mass would be conducted with portions from REFLECTIONS in the reading of the Word portion of the Mass. Prayers should originate with those attending the meeting; especially appropriate would be spontaneous 'prayers of the faithful' based on the feelings each person has upon hearing the meditations and the Scripture. Much, of course, again depends upon the size of groups.

After the Liturgical or para-liturgical celebration, a leader, a guest speaker or a member of the clergy should give an informal talk on a variety of prayer themes for each meeting: the meaning of prayer, types of prayer, what prayer can do, how prayer helped me, why pray, God hears our prayers, etc. Group or individual interest would be limited only by the speakers' ability to spark response.

Close meetings again with readings from REFLECTIONS and the Bible; prayer. Announce what should be done during week to be ready for next meeting: posters, banners, collages, research, readings, between-meeting group discussions, etc.

Format #3

For small group discussion meetings in homes. Have a reading assignment of 1 or 2 passages, inter-related if more than one, between meetings. A full reading of the scriptural references for the particular assignments would be expected. Also members would be urged to study the photography that appears near each reading to be prepared to comment on their reactions to both pictures and words.

At the group meeting a full discussion would be held, chaired by the group leader, on the meaning of the passages, the reaction of each person to the readings and to the photographic

visual-theology. This should be followed by a full development of the scriptural reading and a group discussion of what the particular passage means to them as a group and to their geographic, economic and spiritual place in society.

The normal prayers and informal discussion of any adult discussion group would be used and followed.

SUGGESTIONS FOR PRAYER GROUPS

Prayer Groups

Prayer groups of all kinds and sizes can use REFLECTIONS to advantage for readings, for meditation, for discussion; or as a base from which the individual can speak out on his own commitment and belief.

One passage could act as an opener. Read by a leader, all members of the group would be expected to give "first thought" response and evaluation. Prayer of the Faithful or other personal prayer construction would be based on the passage read. Each member of a prayer group would have a copy of the book and a Bible from which he could add to the proceedings or quietly pray.

REFLECTIONS will fit in well with any prayer group. The mood or use would be up to leaders who sense the need and direction of a particular group. Read a passage aloud and invite verbal personal prayer and evaluation. Or read a passage aloud and invite discussion on prayer meaning, positive themes, ability to provide hope and stimulation.

A reading could be made to an intimate group and each individual would be expected to offer his or her particular thoughts relevant to the passage and perhaps in relation to the particular group. Leader would sum up thoughts and then offer scriptural readings on same theme for meditation prior to the reception of the Eucharist.

Different people could read different passages selected at random. Readings would be slow and evenly paced. The group would then be asked for comment on any common themes underlying readings, any differences, any outstanding feelings pro or con. For this, members should read entire book several times prior to the first meeting to be generally familiar with themes of these meditations.

The full color photography, described as visual-theology, offers leaders an opportunity to present picture thoughts to people. Select a picture and ask for comment. Let each person hold his copy of the book close to himself so he is not distracted. Each looks, for a few minutes, at the selected picture in silence and then without trying to sort thoughts, speaks out on what each feels about the picture. Repeat several times with different pictures.

REFLECTIONS is also appropriate for readings at funeral vigils and funeral services. Prayer and meditation would be invited. These meditations are very effective at Nocturnal Vigils, Novenas and Religious Organization meetings where a spiritual tone is desired.

Pulpit Homily use is a proven asset of these meditations. Most have been used in pulpits with excellent results. They can be used alone as short sermons with impact, or as the core for a longer talk.

The positive, hopeful feeling found in REFLECTIONS makes these passages ideal for any Christian prayer group (silent, vocal, action-oriented) which desires to praise God and be one with Him in prayer.

Photograph by Thomas Trusewicz

The author

Reverend James C. Turro (M.A., S.T.L., S.S.L.)
studied at Catholic University in Washington,
The Biblical Institute in Rome, Columbia University
and New York University. Father Turro is a Professor
of Sacred Scripture at Immaculate Conception
Seminary, Darlington, New Jersey.

Father Turro has written articles for The New
Catholic Encyclopedia, The Jerome Biblical
Commentary, The Old Testament Reading Guides
(Liturgical Press), the Fordham University Pastoral
Psychology Series, a pamphlet on Prayer (Paulist
Press). He has also contributed book reviews to
The Catholic Biblical Quarterly, Theological Studies
and Catholic Historical Review.

In addition to his position as a Professor at the
Archdiocese of Newark Seminary, Father Turro is a
visiting Professor at Mary Rogers College, Maryknoll,
N.Y., visiting Professor of New Testament, La Salle
Graduate Program in Religious Education in
Philadelphia. He was a member of the first Priest
Senate elected in the Archdiocese of Newark. He has
also participated in Sister Formation Programs in
Boston, Philadelphia, Caldwell College, Villa Walsh
and Felician College in New Jersey. He has been
involved in programs for the continuing education of
priests in Harrisburg, Pa., and Douglaston, N.Y.;
gives retreats to Sisters and seminarians each year,
and is a weekend assistant at a suburban parish
in the Archdiocese of Newark.